Chenjing Jiao

Change in Price and Changed Circumstances

A comparative analysis of Chinese, English, German,US laws and internatinoal rules

Studies on Comparative Law

Volume 3

Change in Price and Changed Circumstances

A comparative analysis of Chinese, English, German,US laws and internatinoal rules

by

Chenjing Jiao

SOCIETAS 2013

Bibliographic information published by the Deutsche Nationalbibliothek

The Deutsche Nationalbibliothek lists this publication in the Deutsche Nationalbibliografie; detailed bibliographic data are available in the Internet at http://dnb.dnb.de.

Bibliographische Information der Deutschen Nationalbibliothek

Die Deutsche Nationalbibliothek verzeichnet diese Publikation in der deutschen Nationalbibliographie; detaillierte bibliographische Daten sind im Internet über <http://dnb.ddb.de> abrufbar.

Societas Verlagsgesellschaft KG, Bad Frankenhausen, 2013

ISBN 978-3-944420-02-8

www.societas-verlag.de
www.societas-publishers.com

Table of Contents

A. Introduction

The development of law is affected by certain external factors, such as social, political, technological, economic, and so forth. With the acceleration of globalisation, world economy plays an increasingly significant role. Accordingly, prices, as the basic element of free-market economy,[1] attract much more attention,[2] especially when the price evidently changed after the conclusion of the contract. This put a good deal of stress on contract law and demanded a solution.

The positive law of virtually every country allows for an important exception to the principle that contracts must be performed[3]: unforeseen economic, political and social events can impede or encumber the performance of a contract between its conclusion and execution, eg a monetary devaluation, an economic crisis, armed conflicts, an embargo, an export ban or any kind of unexpected procurement difficulty.[4] As legal excuses for non-performance or damages, these events are carefully classified and governed. Some of them are guided by the concept of common mistake. For instance, parties' errors concerning events before the conclusion of contracts are included in the definition of common

[1] Cf PR Gregory and RC Stuart, *Comparing Economic Systems in the Twenty-First Century* (7th edn, South-Western College Pub 2003).

[2] 'Inflation as measured by the Consumer Price Index first surged in the late1960s and early 1970s to an annual rate of four to five percent, which was then felt to be unacceptably high. Following a slight respite in the mid-1970s, a combination of the second OPEC oil embargo in 1979 and expansionary monetary policy by the Federal Reserve System led to a renewed and even greater surge of inflation, reaching a peak in 1981 when the Consumer Price Index reached an annual rate of fourteen percent'. Cf TR Hurst, 'Inflation, Deflation and Long Term Contractual Relationships Under UCC Section 2-615' [1990] 95 Com LJ 290.

[3] H Leclercq, 'Force Majeure in Chinese Commercial law' [1989] 7 J Energy & Nat Resources L 238.

[4] H Rösler, 'Hardship in German Codified Private Law – In Comparative Perspective to English, French and International Contract Law' [2007] 15(4) ERPL 483.

mistakes in German and English law.[5] Some of them are ruled by *force majeure*[6] which relieves the disadvantaged party of its duty to perform when an event renders that performance impossible. While some of them are regulated in the name of 情势变更 (changed circumstances) in Chinese law[7], frustration of purpose in English law[8], commercial impracticability in US law[9] and the theory of *Wegfall der Geschäftsgrundlage* in German law.[10]

The problem of changed circumstances normally arises in the absence of a contractual clause dealing with this kind of supervening event and will fundamentally alter the equilibrium of the contract. Whilst a change in value, regardless of inflation or currency fluctuation, is the most sensitive one which is particularly acute with respect to long-term contracts. Every national law has to cope with such a problem.

This text seeks to establish whether changes in price should be included in changed circumstances in Chinese law. Because China's present legal system has long been being influenced since the last century by international rules or usage and some countries, especially German[11] and certain other developed countries and the dramatic globali-

---

[5] Cf E McKendrick, *Chitty on contracts – General principles.* (Sweet & Maxwell 2004).

[6] Take Chinese law as an example, *force majeure* is a legal excuse for non-performance as prescribed in article 117 of the Contract Law of the People's Republic of China: 因不可抗力不能履行合同的,根据不可抗力的影响,部分或全部免除责任,但法律另有规定的除外。(A party who was unable to perform a contract due to force majeure is exempted from liability in part or in whole in light of the impact of it, unless it is otherwise provided...).

[7] 情势变更 (changed circumstances) has long been discussed in China but first codified on 24th September 1999. The doctrine of changed circumstances is also used in international rules, like PECL.

[8] The leading case on this subject is *Krell v Henry* [1903] 2 KB 740.

[9] S 2-615 Uniform Commercial Code.

[10] In German law, a fundamental change in circumstances upon which a contract was based can cause the dissolution or adaptation of a contract after the conclusion of a contract. Cf H Rösler, 'Hardship in German Codified Private Law – In Comparative Perspective to English, French and International Contract Law' [2007] 15(4) ERPL 483. This is embodied in s 275 of the German Civil Code (BGB) and further clearly stated in s 313 BGB.

[11] In China, the event when Shen Jiaben was in charge of the revision of Qing Code in 1902 is recognised as the start of modern judicature reform. During that reform, the German codification was adopted. 沈家本 (Shen Jiaben) (1840-1913) is known as the 'father of China's law modernization'. Cf Li Guilian, *Shen Jiaben Nianpuchangbian* (Taibei, Chengwen Press 1992) [李贵连,《沈家本年谱长编》,(台北, 成文出版社,1992)].

sation contributes to a country's legal development, this text will adopt a comparative way at both national and international level.

To discuss change in price, the change of circumstances must first be discussed. Chapter B of this text will outline the development of modern changed circumstances which is rooted in *rebus sic stantibue*. Then, to illustrate the present situation of change of circumstances in China, thereby highlighting the problems around changes in price, a statute and a typical case will be examined. In chapter D, a brief introduction will illustrate the attitudes toward changed circumstances, changes of price and solutions to these issues in English, German and US law found. Aside from these national legal solutions, the general approach to this issue of a series of international instruments, such as the UN Convention on Contracts for the International Sale of Goods ('CISG'), the Principle of European Contract Law ('PECL'), the UNIDROIT principle of International Commercial Contract will be discussed. Since the identification of changes in price is closely related to economics, the International Swaps and Derivatives Association ('ISDA') needs toward the role of changes at an international level will be explored. In chapter E, a comparative analysis will be carried out – between the aforesaid legal systems and that of China, so as to find out whether their findings about change in price can be introduced into Chinese law and to what extent it can be adopted. Finally, the conclusion will offer possible solution that to exclude change in price from the theory of changed circumstances in China is the better way.

B. Rebus Sic Stantibus

Pacta sunt servanda (or the sanctity of contract), which means that what the parties have agreed should normally be respected and upheld[12] is a fundamental and universally accepted principle of the law of contract: '[T]he principle of the sanctity of contracts [...] has always constituted an integral part of most legal systems. These include those systems that are based on Roman law, the Napoleonic Code (eg article 1134) and other European civil codes like German law, as well as Anglo-Saxon Common Law [...]'[13] It requires faithful performance of contractual obligations.

However, with *pacta sunt servanda* kept in mind as a general principle, one should also note that there must be some situations that the circumstances have changed so radical that the performance is fundamentally different from that which was initially promised by the parties. To deal with such problems, the exception of *pacta sunt servanda*, know as *rebus sic stantibue*, was developed.

The doctrine of *rebus sic stantibue*, ie the assumption that matters or circumstances remain in the same state or, every contract is subject to the implied condition (operating as a condition subsequent)[14], was born in medieval Canon law[15] in order to safeguard the axiom of the 'just price'. It was contained in several natural law codifications[16], such as Bavarian Code of 1756, Prussian Code of 1794, and so forth. However, this concept lost currency in Europe, particularly in Germany, during the nineteenth century.

[12] Philips Hong Kong Ltd v Attorney General of Hong Kong (1993) 61 BLR 41.

[13] Liamco v Libya, 12th April 1977, Yearbook Commercial Arbitration (1981).

[14] P Hay, 'Frustration and its Solution in German Law' [1961] 10(4) Am J Comp Law 345.

[15] J Gordley and AT von Mehren, *An introduction to the Comparative Study of Private Law: Readings, Cases, Materials* (Cambridge University Press 2006) 503.

[16] J Gordley, *Foundations of Private Law* (Oxford University Press 2006).

The cause contributing to its demise was firstly that the abuse of this principle threatened the stability of the legal order,[17] or to put it in other words, it seriously went against the ancient maxim *pacta sunt servanda* (or the sanctity of contract). Another reason caused its declines is the rise of the will theories of contract,[18] private autonomy. Parties became free to pursue their personal interests in business; nothing and no one could interfere any more with the free expression of their will.[19] Jurists seemed to forget all the previous conceptions about changed circumstances, *rebus sic stantibus.* Even the two most important codifications of the nineteenth century – the French and German – did not provide remedies if it is because of lack of balance due to a change of circumstances (*rebus sic stantibue*).[20]

This situation lasted for a century and then new perspectives were ready to flourish in contract law. The World War which broke out in the first half of the 20th century caused the world economic crisis and currency devaluation which interested many countries involved in the conflicts, lead jurists to reconsider the whole question of impracticability, changed conditions, just price, and so on.[21] The doctrine of *rebus sic stantibue* gradually established its status and increasingly influence of the field of law, eg it was incorporated in the codification in the United States and embraced by Principles of European Contract Law.

As a member of this globe[22] the People's Republic of China (PRC) goes with the tide and adopt the principle of *rebus sic stantibue* in the form of codification so as to 'protect the lawful rights and interests of contract parties and safeguard social and economic order'.[23]

In spite of such acceptance, the exploration around changed circumstances, even in these countries accepted this theory, has never stopped.[24] At international level, there are still no uniform answers and usage about this issue at international level. For example, the United Nations Convention on Contracts for the International Sale of

---

[17] Ibid.

[18] J Gordley and AT von Mehren, *An introduction to the Comparative Study of Private Law: Readings, Cases, Materials* (Cambridge University Press 2006) 504.

[19] Cf P Gallo, 'Changed Conditions and Problems of Price Adjustment. An Historical and Comparative analysis' [1998] 6 ERPL 285.

[20] Ibid.

[21] Ibid.

[22] This means the event that China went back to United Nations in 1971.

[23] Article 2 of the Contract Law of the PRC.

[24] For example, the limits and relations between changed in circumstances and force majeure, changed circumstances and hardship.

Goods ('CISG') differs from the Principles of European Contract Law ('PECL').[25] What is changed circumstances? When is it applied in different cases and how is the line drawn between unforeseeable price change and commercial risks? Whether changes in price should be a trigger event of applying the doctrine of changed circumstances? The same problems, particularly the changes in price, exist in China as well. In the following part, we will proceed with the present situation of changed circumstances and the deep-seated problems closely related to change in price in China.

---

[25]The CISG specifies the rules dealing with force majeure or hardship rather than clarifying changed circumstances and does not include a provision for a change of fundamental circumstances or the adjustment of contracts, whilst PECL calls its article 6:111 changed circumstances. See H Rösler, 'Hardship in German Codified Private Law – In Comparative Perspective to English, French and International Contract Law' [2007] 15(4) ERPL 483, 504.

C. Changed Circumstances in Chinese Law

I. Changed Circumstances in Contract Law of the PRC

The rule generally applicable in China regarding changed circumstances is to be found in the Supreme People's Court's Interpretations of Certain Issues Concerning the Application of The Contract Law (II)[26] ('Contract Law Interpretation II'), enacted on 24th April, 2009 by the Supreme People's Court. The Article 26 of it specified that:

> 'After the conclusion of the contract, if fundamental circumstances have significantly changed due to unforeseeable, non-force-majeure and non-commercial-risk reasons, to continue the performance of the contract is obviously unfair to one party or cannot fulfil the expectation of the parties, if one party claims for termination or recession of the contract, the People's Court shall determine to terminate or revise the case by taking the case-by-case situations into consideration in lights of the principle of fairness'.[27]

[26]The Supreme People's Court's Interpretation of Certain Issues Concerning the Application of the Contract Law. The Interpretation in this form has the same effect as codified Contract Law in China.

[27]Authors translation of the Contract Law Interpretation II, enforced 13th May 2009.

This is the first time that 'changed circumstances' was incorporated into Contract Law in China.[28] From this article we can see that (a) one party may be excused from performance when a change of circumstances exceeds the contracting parties' expectation and control. 'Changed circumstances' is a legal excuse for non-performance and (b) an event constitutes 'changed circumstances' if it satisfies the following five conditions.[29]

1. Something radically different from that which was in the contemplation of the parties.

Just as the a conctract Law of the PRC states, contract is an agreement between natural persons, legal persons or other organisations with equal standing, for the purpose of establishing, altering, or discharging a relationship of civil rights and obligations.[30] Strictly speaking, the parties shall perform their respective obligations in accordance with the lawfully formed contract and none of them has the rights to arbitrarily modify or terminate the contract, thereby maintaining the contract certainty and fulfilling the contracting parties' expectations.

In this case, to claim an existence of change of circumstances, one must find certain essential circumstances of the contract altered sufficiently that it goes far beyond the obligators' intentions of binding themselves. Some of the scholars in China believe that these circumstances, for example, the serious destruction of the equivalence relation, like serious monetary inflation, the dramatic rise of raw materials and a change in government policies.[31]

---

[28] Cheng Shunzeng, 'Change of Circumstances and Chinese Contract Law system – From the point of the application of Article 26 of Contract Law Interpretation II of the PRC' [2012] 6 Journal of Law Application [程顺增,论情势变更制度与我国合同法体系之契合–以最高法院《关于适用〈中华人民共和国合同法〉若干问题的解释（二）》第26 条的适用为视角,法律适用,2012年第6期].

[29] The main meanings of the 5 conditions are cited from Shi Shangkuan, *The Law of Obligation* (China University of Political Science and Law Press January 2000) [史尚宽,《债法总论》,中国政法大学,2000年1月]. The detailed interpretations are not cited from it.

[30] Article 2 Contract Law of the PRC.

[31] For example, Li Jianwei mentioned this in his civil law training text in 2011.

2. The change of circumstances occurred after the time of conclusion of the contract but before the end of it.

The second condition means that if the event happened prior to the conclusion of the contract, or to put it in other words, a party enters into a contract on the basis of a misapprehension about the facts or the law before the conclusion of the contract, the other party generally should be able to rely on the existence of the contract unless:

Either of the parties may petition the People's Court or an arbitration institution for amendment or cancellation of a contract if:

(a) the contract was concluded due to a material mistake;

(b) the contract was grossly unconscionable at the time of its conclusion.

If a party induced the other party to enter into a contract against its true intention by fraud or duress, or by taking advantage of the other party's hardship, the aggrieved party is entitled to petition the People's Court or an arbitration institution for amendment or cancellation of the contract.[32]

3. Both the event and the nature of the event are unforeseeable

The third condition contains more than one meaning. To start with, the change of circumstances should not have reasonably been taken into account by contracting parties. That is, changed circumstances cannot be invoked if the matter would have been foreseen and taken into account by a reasonable man in the same situation, by a person who is neither unduly optimistic or pessimistic, nor careless of his own interests. Then, the circumstance itself is unforeseeable. It, however, excludes not only *force majeure* which means any objective circumstance that is unforeseeable, unavoidable and insurmountable[33] but also commercial risks.

[32] Article 54 Contract Law of the PRC.

[33] Article 177 Contract Law of the PRC.

4. It is not due to the contracting parties' fault

If a party engaged in any of the following conducts in the course of concluding a contract, thereby causing loss to the other party, it shall be liable for damages:

(a) negotiating in bad faith under the pretext of concluding a contract;

(b) intentionally concealing a material fact relating to the conclusion of the contract or supplying false information;

(c) any other conduct which violates the principle of good faith.[34]

However, if the failure is due to the party's fault who relying on it, change in circumstances cannot be applicable, that is to say, changed circumstances cannot be relied on when it is self-induced.

5. It has frustrated the original basis of the contract so that the continuing performance would obviously render unfairness.

Any contract, especially one of long duration, is made in a particular social and economic situation which may not last – it is this notion which underlies the ancient '*clausula rebus sic stantibus*'. Nevertheless, only a subsequent change in the economic context does not give a party the right to have the contract revised or terminated. The 'changed circumstances' only comes into play when it has brought about a major imbalance in the contract; if the contract is completely overturned by events, so that although it can still be performed, this will involve completely exorbitant costs for one of the parties.

This final codification of the most controversial issues in drafting the Contract Law reflects the modern trend that giving the court some power to moderate the rigours of freedom and sanctity of contract. This is because in practice, an increasing number of contracting parties have foreseen the possibilities that certain situations may cause the performance of the contract to become much more onerous when they enter into it and try to prevent the possible problems using some clauses like *force majeure, hardship* and so forth. However, the experience

[34] Article 42 Contract Law of the PRC.

suggests that frequently the parties are not sufficiently sophisticated to make provisions to prevent the following complex situations; or they insert terms and conditions which do not cover every eventuality. It can also happen that the operation of the clause itself runs into some unforeseen difficulty.[35] Consequently, there are some cases in which the court would intervene in the contractual relationship so as to give effect to the demands of fairness and justice.

II. Changed Circumstances in practice

In fact, cases in China have no legal force, as opposed to the precedents' in the UK. However, there is a case *Wuhan Gas Company (WGC) v Chongqing Testing Instrument Factory (CTIF)*[36] in China shown the acceptance and application for changed circumstances in the absence of legislation of change of circumstances.

In that case, WGC entered into a cooperation contract of technology transfer on J2.5 gas table assembly line and a supplemental contract (transfer contract) in September 1987 with CTIF. At the same time, the parties also signed a purchase contract of J2.5 gas meter parts and a supplemental contract (purchase contract) that CTIF supply WGC with 70,000 sets of J2.5 gas meters made of aluminium amounting to a total sum of RMB 4,011,000, RMB 57.3 per set. The contract provided that CTIF should deliver 30.000 sets in 1988 and 40,000 sets in 1989 to WGC.

The parties performed the transfer contract without problem, whereas the purchase contract caused a dispute. Several months after the purchase contract was concluded, the price of aluminium was drastically adjusted by the PRC from RMB 4,400-4,600 per ton to 16,000 per ton. Consequently, the cost of producing the gas meters rapidly increased to RMB 79.22 per set and the suggested selling price given by the relevant commodity price department was RMB 83 per set. Based on such dramatic changes, CTIF contacted WGC several times to clarify the situation and to ask them to modify the agreed price or rescind it. The final offer was RMB 75.5 per set, regardless of the profits. WGC refused, insisting on performing the original purchase

[35] H Beale and O Lando, *Principles of European Contract Law, Parts I and II* (Kluwer Law International Press 2000) 323.

[36] Plaintiff sued Defendant in 1989, while the dispute was finally resolved in 1992.

contract. After CTIF stopped delivering the gas meters, WGC sued CTIF.

At trial, Wuhan Intermediate People's Court entered a judgment which was not in favour of CTIF. The Court held that the two contracts which were concluded on the ground of voluntariness, fairness and sufficient consideration were made of lawful content and therefore were valid. Consequently CTIF was made fully liable for its contractual obligation.

On appeal, the High People's Court of Hubei Province reversed the former judgement. In remanding the case for further proceeding, the High Court was of the opinion that if during the performance of the contract, there was a material change that the parties could not have foreseen at the time when the parties made the contract, and if continuing performance would cause manifestly unfair result, the doctrine of changed circumstances should be applicable to maintain the notion of fairness.[37]

The Supreme People's Court endorsed the opinion of the High People's Court of Hubei Province by its No 27 letter of judicial instruction issued on 6th March 1992.[38] The Supreme People's Court held that for the purposes of the instant case, due to the change in circumstances that could not be foreseen and prevented by the parties during the performance of the contract, it would be obviously unfair if CIFT was asked to fulfil its obligations according to the original contract.

In 1993, the Supreme People's Court further clarified that if due to the reasons for which none of the parties may be blamed, an unpredictable change in the circumstances on which the contract is based is so essential that it would be obviously unfair to enforce the original contract, the people's courts may, upon the request of the parties, modify or dissolve the contract under the doctrine of *rebus sic stantibus*.[39]

It reflected the view that if the facts contradict the will of the parties' consensual expectation and drastically change the risks the parties could reasonable estimate before they entered into a contract, it is not

---

[37] Cf Kong X, *Comments and Theoretical Study on Difficult Cases of the Contract Law* (Revised edn, People's Court Press 2000) 396.

[38] The letter of judiciary letter from the Supreme People's Court is normally used by the Supreme People's Court to answer legal questions raised by a High Court concerning interpretation and application of specific law or regulation in a particular case.

[39] Cf Supreme People's Court, 'Minutes on 1993 National Symposium on Trials of Economic Cases', May 6. 1993 Fa Fa (1993) No. 8.

the real content of the contract. The parties, therefore, were entitled to terminate or partially discharge the contract by way of litigation, thereby achieving their real intention and protected their expected interest and the real justice and fairness. Although statute law is the legal basis in China, this case has a far-reaching impact on the issue of changed circumstances, especially when there was no statute thereto.[40]

III. The Problems around Change in Price reflected in the foregoing case

On the surface, the case was fairly judged because it prevented the severe risk of bankruptcy of one party by modifying the price of the binding contract. However, it should be noted that there are some deep-seated questions arising from coping with price change by means of applying the principle of changed circumstances in China.

1. Discretion

It is understandable that whatever the significance of the sanctity of contract is in legal theory, the doctrine of change of circumstances in practice has demonstrated that on many occasions this principle may lead to the opposite of its original intention.[41] Thus, it is tempered by the principle of *rebus sic stantibus*. The courts' entitlement to interfere with contractual relationships for the purpose of achieving final fairness is necessary to some degree.

Nevertheless, can judges be empowered to modify the key terms and conditions such as price?

Article 26 of Contract Law Interpretation II should not indicate that '*the People's Court shall determine to terminate or revise the case by taking the case-by-case situations into consideration in light of the principle of fairness*'. Therefore, the answer is positive. The courts are entitled to affirm a new price in the event of change in price, regardless of the contractual parties' true intention. But contracts are the products of the parties' consensual intention and the Contract Law of the

[40] Because the cases are not published as they are in the UK, the formal reasoning procedure of the judges cannot usually be obtained. The relevant information obtained on this topic mainly comes from communications with a number of judges.

[41] D Maskow, 'Hardship and Force Majeure' [1992] 40 Am J Comp L 657.

PRC also states that a lawfully formed contract is protected by law.[42] Can a mandatory modification be placed upon the contract determined by the parties of their own accord? How do the parties' to fulfil the expected future of their contract if their true intention does not matter?

The balance between the power of law and all the legal rights owned to a person is disturbed. Consequently, it is not impossible that discretion could be abused due to the absence of uniform and clear rules relating to the extent of 'unreasonable price changes' and how to exercise discretion.

To this extent, incorporating change of price into changed circumstances essentially goes against the original aim of achieving real justness.

2. Force majeure and change of circumstances

Force majeure, according to article 153 of the General Principles of the Civil Law of the PRC, means unforeseeable, unavoidable and insurmountable objective conditions. There is no official detailed scopt of *force majeure*. However, generally speaking, it consists of three aspects: (a) natural disasters, such as earthquake, tsunami, flood, drought, etc; (b) social events such as war, strike, government restrant or policy and so forth; (c) human-error accidents.[43] Thus, by comparing the definition of *force majure* and article 26 of Contract Law Interpretation II, it is clear that change in circumstances and *force majeure* are different from each other in Chinese law.

In terms of the aforesaid case, if the information is more carefully reviewed, it is clear that change in price is due to the state adjustment. In other words, it resulted from a government policy which belongs to the range of *force majeure* rather than 'change of circumstances'. If it was understandable at that particular stage of economic development, then the status quo that they are always mixed together is a cause for concern.

3. The place for change in price

It is very difficult, if not impossible, to draw a line between *rebus sic stantibus* and normal commercial risk. Particularly difficult to separate

[42] Article 8 Contract Law of the PRC.

[43] Zhang Tan, 'On the Limit to the Principle of Changes in Situation' [1996] 5 Hebei Law [张坦,论对情势变更原则的限制,河北法学1996年第5期].

change in price which can trigger the application of the doctrine of change of circumstance from regular commercial risk. That's one of the several reasons why *rebus sic stantibus* was ultimately dropped from the final draft of the Contract Law of the PRC.[44] Now, since there is an actual legislative endorsement, distinguishing change in price is of great importance to its further use of *rebus sic stantibus.*

In the previously-discussed case we discussed, increases in the cost of performing an executor made that contract unprofitable to one party. A similar issue may arise where the general process of inflation reduces in real terms the profit which that party expected to obtain under the contract.[45] In this instance, is it reasonable to apply *rebus sic stantibus*?

Since these questions arise from the attitude towards change in price in China, it is useful to examine other continues (I) English law, (II) German law (III) US law and (IV) international rules which have influenced Chinese legal system.

[44]Cf Sun Lihai, *Selection of Legislative Materials of the Contract Law of the People's Republic of China* (Law Press 1999) 54-55.

[45]E Peel and G Treitel, *The Law of Contract* (12th edn, Sweet & Maxwell 2007).

D. Change in Price and Changed Circumstances in some other Legal Systems

I. English Law

The starting point is the 'absolute contract' rule in English law. The firmly settled orthodox principle of contract law is that 'the conditions of the contract must be strictly performed'.[46] The reason is that 'In essence, a contract is a promise or undertaking in respect of which legal contractual obligation has been assumed by means which the law recognises as effective for that purpose'[47] and 'A promise is a statement by which one person commits to some future beneficial performance, or the beneficial withholding of a performance, in favour of another person.'[48]

It has been a traditionally accepted feature of English law that only bargain promises, that is, 'promise' supported by consideration, are binding.[49] In other words, in certain circumstances, a bargain promise which has been made and accepted may still not be binding. That is, there are exceptions[50] to absolute contract.

---

[46] Arcos v Ronaasen [1933] AC 470.

[47] B Coote, *Contract as Assumption* (Hart Publishing 2010) 42.

[48] M Hogg, *Promises and Contract law: comparative perspectives* (Cambridge University Press 2011) 6.

[49] A Burrows, *Understanding the law of Obligations: 'Dividing the Law of Obligations'* (Hart Publishing 1998).

[50] There are different 'exceptions' such as impossibility, frustration, and so on. Impossibility encompasses a wide range of situations: destruction of the subject-matter of the contract, its unavailability (due, for instance, if a ship or aircraft is requisitioned by the government), or death or incapacity of a party who had undertaken a personal obligation. Cf H Beale, B Fauvarque-cosson, J Rutgers,

Some of the exceptions are exemplified by three early cases of *Westminster v Clarke*[51], *Hyde v The Dean of Windsor*[52], and *Williams v Floyd*[53]. However, English law has never known the medieval excuse of *rebus sic stantibus* doctrine. It tackles the foregoing exceptions in the name of frustration, which sets the contract aside if factual or legal circumstances have changed to such an extent that the performance of the parties' contractual obligations has turned out to be drastically different from what they had initially intended.[54] In *Davis Contractors Ltd v Fareham UDC* Lord Radcliffe put the matter thus:

> 'Frustration occurs whenever the law recognises that, without default of either party, a contractual obligation has become incapable of being performed because the circumstances in which performance is called for would render it a thing radically different from that which was undertaken by the contract. Non haec in foedera veni. It was not this that I promised to do'.[55]

Therefore, the frustration mechanism only comes into play 'when the contract is completely overturned by events, so that although it still can be performed, this will involve completely exorbitant costs for one of the parties'[56].

Such modern doctrine of frustration, of which at least five theories of the basis have been put forward at various times[57], is based on *Taylor v Caldwell* in which the judge Blackburn stated that

> '[...] it appears that the parties must from the beginning have known that it could not be fulfilled unless when the time for the fulfilment of the contract arrived some particular specified thing continued to exist, so that, when entering into the contract, they must have contemplated such

D Tallon and S Vogenauer, *Cases, Materials and Text on Contract Law* (2nd edn, Hart Publishing 2010) 1093.

[51] Dyer 276, pl 186, 73, Eng Rep 59, 63 (1536).

[52] Cro Eliz 552, 78 Eng Rep 798 (1597).

[53] W Jones 179, 82 Eng Rep 309 (1863).

[54] GH Treitel, *Frustration and Force Majeure* (2nd edn, Sweet & Maxwell 2004).

[55] Davis Contractors Ltd v Fareham UDC [1956] AC 696; National Carriers Ltd v Panalpina Northern Ltd [1981] AC 675 by Hailsham LJ: 'it is the formulation I personally prefer'.

[56] H Beale and O Lando, *Principles of European Contract Law, Parts I and II* (Kluwer Law International Press 2000) 325.

[57] National Carriers Ltd v Panalpina Northern Ltd [1981] AC 675.

continuing existence as the foundation of what was to be done. [...] [I]n contracts in which the performance depends on the continued existence of a given person or thing, a condition is implied that the impossibility of performance arising from the perishing of the person or thing shall excuse the performance.'[58]

Of numerous cases dealing with frustration, the leading one on the subject is the famous case of *Krell v Henry*[59] in 1903, which concerned a party Krell who had rented a room at the price of £ 75 in order to watch the passing coronation procession of Edward VII. The coronation was indefinitely postponed for the king fell ill. The hirer refused to pay the rest £ 50 for the room. Thus the owner sued for breach of contract.

In the judgment, Vaughan Williams LJ stated that 'the taking place of those processions on the days proclaimed along the proclaimed route, which passed 56A, Pall Mall, was regarded by both contracting parties as the foundation of the contract [...]' Even though 'the illness of the King did not make the execution of the contract 'impossible', the cancellation of the parade merely frustrated the purpose for which both men originally contracted.'[60] Accordingly, the courts discharged both parties from further performance of the contract, leaving the parties as they were.

This judgement indicates that English law takes an 'all-or-nothing' approach[61] towards frustration case, that is, the court has no discretion to qualify the contract for the purpose of doing what seems to it just and reasonable.[62]

With respect to change in price, 'English authorities do not support the view that inflation is a ground of frustration',[63] both inflation and currency fluctuation are not legal excuses leading to an application of frustration of purpose in English law.

In *British Movietonews v London and District Cinemas*,[64] the defendants, film exhibitors, entered into an agreement with the plain-

[58]Taylor v Caldwell [1863] 122 ER 309.

[59][1903] 2 KB 740.

[60]Krell v Henry [1903] 2 KB 740.

[61]H Beale and O Lando, *Principles of European Contract Law, Parts I and II* (Kluwer Law International Press 2000) 325.

[62]British Movietonews v London and District Cinemas [1952] AC 166.

[63]E Peel and GH Treitel, *The Law of Contract* (12th edn, Sweet & Maxwell 2007) 945.

[64][1952] AC 166.

tiffs, film distributors, in July 1941 for the purpose of exhibiting news reel films. The agreement was terminable by four weeks' notice. In May 1943, the parties to the original agreement made a supplemental agreement containing conditions dictated by existing war circumstances. The agreement was to remain in full force and effect until the Cinematograph Film (Control) Order 1943 was cancelled and thereafter for any unexpired period stipulated by the original agreement. In 1948, the conditions in which the agreement of 1943 had been made had changed and the exhibitors attempted to terminate the agreement, although the order of 1943 still remained in force under a different statute.

The House of Lords held that the exhibitors were not entitled to give notice terminating the principal agreement. The House of Lord further mapped out the general view that a contract would cease to bind if a 'fundamentally different situation' were to emerge. This may refer back to the reasons previously given in the passage that 'a wholly abnormal rise or fall in price, a sudden depreciation of currency' are unpredicted turns of events which do not frustrate a contract thereby enabling the court to substitute its notion of what is 'just and reasonable' because 'this does not in itself affect the bargain they have made'[65].

Another well-known case concerning change in price and frustration is *Wates Ltd v Greater London Council*[66], in which a building contract to a certain degree protected the contractor against inflation by means of a clause. While the court stated 'Things may have turned out differently from what the parties contemplated in that inflation increased, not at a trot or at a canter, but at a gallop. But the difference in degree or tempo [the inflation which occurred was of the order of 20-25%] was not so radical a difference from the decision contemplated and provided for as to frustrate the contract'.[67]

More recently, in 1996, in *Gore District Council v Power Co Limited*[68], although the normal cost was 12.3 times higher than some 68 years ago when the contract was concluded, Barker J pointed out that the agreement was intended to be perpetual, including the respective bargaining powers of the parties and the benefits and burdens of the

---

[65] British Movietonews v London and District Cinemas [1952] AC 166 at 185 by Simon LJ.

[66] (1983) 25 BLR 1 (CA).

[67] British Movietonews v London and District Cinemas [1952] AC 166 at 185 by Simon LJ.

[68] [1996] 1 NZLR 58.

contract, because 'the words of the agreement are clear. It is difficult to imagine a clearer way a drafter could impose a permanent obligation than to say 'the provision of this deed shall be binding on [the parties] for all time hereafter'. Had the parties wished to make the agreement determinable on reasonable notice, it is safe to assume that they would have done so'[69]. Hence, the judgment denied the possible effect of inflation on the enforceability of the contract. Even though some may argue that Lord Roskill stated in *National Carriers Ltd v Panalpina Northern Ltd* that the inflation is one of the 'circumstances in which the doctrine of frustration has been invoked, sometimes with success, sometimes without',[70] inflation generally is not recognised as an event that can be classified as a trigger event of frustration in the English law.[71]

In respect of currency fluctuations, *Multiservice Bookbinding Ltd v Marden*[72] illustrated that a debtor whose obligations are defined by reference to a change in currency cannot avoid liability to pay in full merely because the pound has fallen in value in relation to that currency by an unexpectedly large change.[73]

II. German Law

In terms of the prerequisites of changed circumstances (*Wegfall der Geschäftsgrundlage*), the German law is not too dissimilar to the English law: the English case law on frustration asks for a 'fundamentally different situation', the German law requires a fundamental change in 'circumstances upon which a contract was based'.[74] Not any fundamental change will suffice. It must be unreasonable to hold the party bound to its duty in the German rule. The courts commonly and until today define fundamental circumstances to be 'perceptions shared by

[69] Gore District Council v Power Co Limited [1996] 1 NZLR 58.

[70] [1981] AC 675.

[71] Even though the judgment of *Staffordshire Area Health Authority v South Staffordshire Water Works Co* [1978] All ER 769 supported the party who claimed the inflation was unfair, it is not based on reason that the inflation should lead to that result and it is 'a widely criticised judgment'. Cf A Ringwood, 'Terminating a Contract' [1996] NZLJ 204.

[72] [1979] Ch 84.

[73] E Peel and GH Treitel, *The Law of Contract* (12th edn, Sweet & Maxwell 2007).

[74] H Rösler, 'Hardship in German Codified Private Law – In Comparative Perspective to English, French and International Contract Law' [2007] 15(4) ERPL 483, 506.

both parties as evident at the closing of the contract, or perceptions of one party, discernible to and not objected to by the other party, of the existence, present or future, of certain circumstances that form the basis of their willingness to contract'.[75]

However, the solution to change of circumstances and change in price in German law are relatively broader.

The German legislator of 1896 did not adopt the medieval Canon law doctrine of *rebus sic stantibus*. This equitable concept had lost appeal in the 19th century and until the 1920s.[76] Just like Hannes Rösler described:

> 'The omission had to be reconsidered between 1920 and November 1923, the month when the currency reform ended Post-World War I hyperinflation that had struck the Weimar Republic. At the end of 1921, prices were 35 times higher than before the war. And a year later they had risen to a level that was 1.475times higher. In less than two years the price of a stamp of 20 Pfenning rose to 500 Trillion Mark.
>
> To counteract the effects of currency devaluation upon private contracts, the then highest German court (the Reichsgericht – RG) first resorted to applying a provision dealing with the impossibility of performance. But, in 1922, the RG changed tack. It stated that the rules governing impossibility were not apt to deal with the situation. Instead, it started applying the concept of change of fundamental circumstances (or a collapse of the basis of the contract, as some also translate).'[77]

Today, the doctrine of changed circumstances is incorporated in German Civil Code (BGB). The following is an official translation of s 313 BGB on the 'Interference with the basis of the transaction':[78]

> (1) If circumstance upon which a contract was based have materially changed after conclusion of the contract and if

---

[75] H Rösler, 'Changed and unforeseen circumstances in German and international contract law', [2008] 5 SLR 47.

[76] Ibid.

[77] Ibid., 48-49.

[78] S 313 German Civil Code (BGB).

> the parties would not have concluded the contract or would have done so upon different terms if they had foreseen that change, adaptation of the contract may be claimed in so far as, having regard to all the circumstances of the specific case, in particular the contractual or statutory allocation of risk, it cannot reasonably be expected that a party should continue to be bound by the contract in its unaltered form.
>
> (2) If material assumptions have become the basis of the contract subsequently turn out to be incorrect, they are treated in the same way as a change in circumstances.
>
> (3) If adaptation of the contract is not possible or cannot be reasonable imposed on one party, the disadvantaged party may terminate the contract. In the case of a contract for the performance of a recurring obligation, the right to terminate is replaced by the right to terminate on notice.

Based on the development mentioned above, it is not wrong to say that it was the change in price (currency devaluation) that directly led to the re-emergence of modern changed circumstances. The following statement of a case[79] fully reflected the re-rise procedure during that period.

> 'In May 1919, one of several owners of a spinning mill agreed to sell his part ownership. The ownership was to be transferred on 1 January 1920 in exchange for one half of the agreed purchasing price. The second half was to be paid in the first months of 1921. Between May 1919 and the beginning of 1920, however, the purchasing power of the currency fell by 80 per cent. The price one party had agreed to pay no longer stood in any relation to the value of the other party's performance. The parties had agreed upon the previous May.[80] The case came before the then highest German court (the Reichsgericht – RG) in 1922. Since no suitable provision in the BGB was available, the RG first resorted to applying a provision dealing with the impossibility

[79] H Rösler, 'Hardship in German Codified Private Law – In Comparative Perspective to English, French and International Contract Law' [2007] 15(4) ERPL 483, 491.

[80] Simplified summary of the judgment in RGZ 103, 328.

> of performance – among rebus sic stantibus – on a concept of economic impossibility. But in its judgment rendered in 1923, the RG turned towards the principle of fundamental change.[81] In creating this subsidiary concept the RG relied heavily on the German scholar Oertmann, whose doctrine of the 'basis of transaction' (Geschäftsgrundlage) was published in 1921.'

In the case outlined above, the *Reichsgericht (RG)* came to the decision that a change in values of the agreed price could also amount to an unforeseen and fundamental change in circumstances, if the parties had assumed the balance of performance and price to be the basis of the contract. Therefore, a case of detrimental change in value of a performance of an agreed exchange led to the first judicial recognition of the doctrine of change of circumstances under the old BGB.[82]

Nevertheless, the situations seen from a present-day perspective are different to a large extent. From s 313 BGB we can see that the possibility not only to end contracts in case of changed circumstances, but also the possibility to modify and adjust contracts to the new situation[83] on the principle of good faith is quite widely admitted in Germany.[84] Such a case (outlined above) could fall into the realm of application of s 313 BGB, but the standard consequence of a significant upward adjustment of the purchasing price would hardly be considered as a reasonable result for the buyer in light of the rapid deterioration in value the currency suffered in the early 1920s. An ordinary change in purchasing power, however, cannot result in an adjustment of contract. It is one of the founding principle of a monetary economy that a debt is defined as a specific sum and not as a fluid value. The obligor hence bears the risk of inflation in all but the most severe cases.[85]

---

[81] RGZ 103, 328, 332.

[82] H Rösler, 'Hardship in German Codified Private Law – In Comparative Perspective to English, French and International Contract Law' [2007] 15(4) ERPL 483, 492.

[83] JP Dawson, 'Judicial Revision of Frustrated Contracts' [1983] 63 BUL Rev 1039.

[84] S 242 BGB; Cf P Gallo, 'Changed Conditions and Problems of Price Adjustment. An Historical and Comparative analysis' [1998] 6 ERPL 285.

[85] H Rösler, 'Hardship in German Codified Private Law – In Comparative Perspective to English, French and International Contract Law' [2007] 15(4) ERPL 483, 492.

III. US Law

As a basic premise of the common law, the Latin dictum *pacta sunt servanda* commands that contracts should be performed absolutely.[86] It tolerates no deviation from the obligations set forth in the terms of the contract.[87] This view assumed that when the parties contracted to perform, performance was to be enforced exactly as written.[88] In other words, contracts were strictly enforced so that where there was an unqualified undertaking, the duty perform was not discharged by the occurrence of an unforeseen event which renders said performance impossible.[89] This theme is continually echoed by the judiciary.[90]

Because the rigid application of this doctrine of strict performance proved unworkable sometimes, by the mid-1800s, this doctrine was firstly altered in *Taylor v Caldwell* to include impossibility as a defense[91] and then developed through the English case *Krell v Henry*.[92] In 1916, the California Supreme Court extended this doctrine by introducing the test of impracticability as a measure of determining impossibility, thus excusing performance. The first case in United States is *Mineral Park Land v Howard*[93] in which the rule was stated 'a thing is impossible in legal contemplation when it is not practicable; and a thing is impracticable when it can only be done at an excessive and unreasonable cost'.[94]

The significance of *Mineral Park* is far more than the test we mentioned. It is one of the few pre-UCC cases in impossibility where the defense of increased cost was held. It proved a rule that 'the courts

---

[86]BS Garner, *Black's Law Dictionary* (5th edn, West Pub Co 1979).

[87]P Walter, 'Commercial Impracticability in Contracts' [1987] 61(2) St John's L Review 225.

[88]Cf A Farnsworth , *Contracts* (Little, Brown 1982).

[89]WD Hawkland, 'The Energy Crisis and Section 2-615 of the Uniform Commercial Code' [1974] 79 Com LJ 75.

[90]Eleventh Circuit in Cook v Deltona Corp [1985] 753 F 2d 1552 (11th Cir). The court stated: 'Contracts are born of the need for certainty. They are the merchant's exchange of serendipity for serenity, the deal upon which he can rely, for better or worse, months or years hence. A contract is insurance against change.'

[91]Taylor v Caldwell [1863] 122 ER 309. US law is closely related to English law. Cf Schmitt MA and Wollschlager BA, 'Commercial Impracticability: Making the Impracticable Practicable' (1976) 81 Com LJ 9; Walter P, 'Commercial Impracticability in Contracts' [1987] 61(2) St John's L Review 225.

[92][1903] 2 KB 740.

[93]172 Cal 289, 156 P 458 (1916).

[94]Ibid.

rarely accepted the impossibility in cases involving increased cost of performance except in cases involving increased cost of exceptional magnitude'[95] by providing that 'To all fair intents, it was impossible for defendants to take it. [...] We do not mean to intimate that the defendants could excuse themselves by showing the existence of conditions which would make the performance of their obligation more expensive than they had anticipated, or which would entail a loss upon them. But, where the difference in cost is so great as here, and has the effect as found, of making performance impracticable, the situation is not different from that of a total absence of earth and gravel'.[96] The development of the doctrine of impracticability had opened the way to new possibilities of redress also in cases of price increase, inflation and so on.[97]

Some other cases like *City of Vernon v City of Los Angeles*[98], *Dillon v United States*[99] also improved this rule that inflation may trigger the application of theory in case of impracticability in the US before UCC.

Nonetheless, it appeared that the strains which had been placed upon the application of the impossibility were too loose and the courts would take a more relaxed view concerning application of the impossibility. As the law gradually evolved from the rule of absolute liability to the standard of impossibility, the primary focus of attention turned to the objective criterion of practicability.[100] Consequently, the Uniform Commercial Code ('UCC') was brought in at the right moment. Section 2-615[101] deliberately speaks of performance which has become 'commercial impracticable' rather than using 'impossible'. Further-

[95]TR Hurst, 'Inflation, Deflation and Long Term Contractual Relationships Under UCC Section 2-615' [1990] 95 Com LJ 290.

[96]Ibid., at 293, 156 P 459-60.

[97]Mineral Park Land v Howard [1916] 172 Cal 289, 156 P 458

[98][1955] 45 Cal 2d 710, 290 P 2d 841.

[99][1957] 156 F Supp 719 (Ct Cl).

[100]Cf P Walter, 'Commercial Impracticability in Contracts' [1987] 61(2) St John's L Review 225.

[101]UCC s 2-615 'Excuse by Failure of Presupposed Conditions': "Except so far as a seller may have assumed a greater obligation and subject to s. 2-614 on substituted performances:

(a) Delay in delivery or non-delivery in whole or in part by a seller... is not a breach of his duty under a contract for sale if performance as agreed has been made impracticable by the occurrence of a contingency the non-occurrence of which was a basic assumption on which the contract was made or by compliance in good faith with any applicable foreign or domestic governmental regulation or order whether or not it later proves to be invalid.

more, it lists the elements of triggering an application of commercial impracticalbility as:

(a) the seller must not have assumed the risk of some unknown contingency;

(b) the non-occurrence of the contingency must have been a basic assumption underlying the contract;

(c) the occurrence of that contingency must have made performance commercially impracticable.[102]

Commercial impracticability is thus formally codified. Despite all of this, the United States courts generally have refused to alter contract prices which have become financially oppressive to one party after a contract has been signed.[103] For instance, since the 1960s, promisors increasingly have sought judicial relief from burdensome contracts. Rising rates of inflation and OPEC price hikes have contributed significantly to this trend. Although several doctrines are potentially applicable, the courts generally have analysed these cases on the basis of commercial impracticability, and almost without exception, they have refused to grant any relief when the promisor's sole complaint has been increased cost of performances.[104] One reason for this reluctance is the difficulty of framing a satisfactory remedy because the normal remedy for commercial impracticability is to excuse or release the promisor from further performance. Discharging a party merely because performance

---

(b) Where the causes mentioned in paragraph (a) affect only a part of the seller's capacity to perform, he must allocate production and deliveries among his customers but may at his option include regular customers not then under contract as well as his own requirements for further manufacture. He may so allocate in any manner which is fair and reasonable.

(c) The seller must notify the buyer seasonably that there will be delay or non-delivery and, when allocation is required under paragraph (b), of which estimated quota thus made available for the buyer.

The Restatement (Second) of Contracts ('Restatement') provided the same meanings in Section 261 of the Restatement as well".

[102] Iowa Elec Light & Power Co [1978] 467 F Supp 129 at 134.

[103] L Stevenson Conrad, 'Bernina Distributors, Inc. v Bernina Sewing Machine Co.: New Grounds for Commercial Impracticability Based on Currency Exchange Rates under Uniform Commercial Code Section 2-615' [1983] NCJ Int'l L & Com Reg 117.

[104] S 2-615 UCC, Official Comment 4.

becomes unprofitable would encourage litigation and tend to undermine the sanctity of contract.[105]

Several US decisions, however, have considered it possible not only to end contractual relationships in case of changed circumstances but also to modify and adjust them to the new situation.[106] The *Alcoa*[107] court, however, embraced the goals of the UCC and Restatement drafters, and its views provide an alternative to the prevailing strict approach to impracticability problems by means of changing the price formula so that it would reflect Alcoa's actual non-labour production cost.[108]

IV. International rules and trends

Given the globalization, the dominant manner in which the theory of changed circumstances is regulated does affect the final decision of individual countries. In spite of the differences between national rules, attempts have been made harmonise the solutions so as to make the international business conventions and usage more accessibly providing greater juridical security for business people.

The needs of international commercial practice break down the barriers produced by the different legal systems, such as civil law, common law, Muslim law, or some other law.[109] In effect, certain rules at international level have been undoubtedly had an effect on the international business.

The most well-recognised is CISG. The CISG has no rule on changed circumstances. Although some Chinese scholars consider article 79 of CISG is to be concerned the aforesaid principle. Not only the distinction between hardship and force majeure but also the clear wording and

[105]TR Hurst, 'Inflation, Deflation and Long Term Contractual Relationships Under UCC Section 2-615' [1990] 95 Com LJ 290, 297.

[106]City of La Follette v La Follette Water, Light and Tel Co 252 F. 762; National presto Industries Inc v Unites States [1964] 338 F. 2nd 99; Alumium Co of America v Essex Group Inc [1980] 499 F Supp 53 (WP Pa).

[107]Aluminium Company of America v Essex Group Inc [1980] 499 F Supp 53 (WD Pa).

[108]SW Hubbard, 'Relief from Burdensome Long-term Contracts: Commercial Impracticability, Frustration of Purpose, Mutual Mistake of Fact, and Equitable Adjustment' [1982] 47 Mo L Rev 79; Under s 2-615 UCC various options can be adopted.

[109]H Veytia, 'The Requirement of Justice and Equity in Contracts' [1995] 69 Tul L Rev 1191.

intention of article 79 CISG speaks against a broad interpretation.[110] Among these opinions as to the proper interpretation of it, the leading one is that 'the CISG has deliberately refrained from laying down any provision (and not only omitted) in regard to the change of circumstances'[111]. CISG is unwilling to give the judiciary such wide discretion, which would lead to a great deal of instability. This consideration is of real worth because civil law system differs from the common law system much as one national law system differs from another even though they belong to one law system.

On the other hand, the UNIDROIT Principles of International Commercial Contracts (hereinafter UNIDROIT Principles)[112] provide a mechanism whereby, if certain requirements are realised, a court may adapt the obligation to the changed circumstances or even terminate the contractual relationship.[113] This mechanism is aimed at dealing with exceptional change of conditions which is so extreme that it would be manifestly unjust to hold the obligor to the contract.

Similarly, article 6:111 of Principles of European Contract Law ('PECL') provided this content. Consequently, under the general duty of good faith, the party which will suffer the hardship must initiate the negotiation within a reasonable time. If the negotiations do not succeed, either of the parties may bring the matter before the court. The court will intervene with wide powers, either terminating the contract or modifying particular terms. However, this is only in the last resort.[114] Even if there are no particular provisions specifying how to take change in price into account separately, in accord with the purpose of this general rule, it is not impossible to rule it if necessary.

---

[110] Rösler H, 'Hardship in German Codified Private Law – In Comparative Perspective to English, French and International Contract Law' [2007] 15(4) ERPL 483, 503.

[111] H Beale, B Fauvarque-cosson, J Rutgers, D Tallon and S Vogenauer, *Cases, Materials and Text on Contract Law* (2nd edn, Hart Publishing 2010).

[112] UNIDROIT Principles are not intended to form a binding international convention, but rather are meant to be used both as a model in the drafting of international contracts and in the determination of the applicable law. Cf H Veytia, 'The Requirement of Justice and Equity in Contracts' [1995] 69 Tul L Rev 1191.

[113] Relevant content is contained in a section of UNIDROIT Principles called Hardship (Article 6.2.1, 6.2.2 at 6.2.3).

[114] H Beale and O Lando, *Principles of European Contract Law, Parts I and II* (Kluwer Law International Press 2000) 326.

E. Analysis: Which solution suits China better

The legal norms and case law provide for quite different answers to the question that how to deal with change in price.

At international level, under the UNIDROIT Principles and PECL, the doctrine of changed circumstances is contained and the judges have the same power of readjustment. While CISG refuse to incorporate changed circumstances, even the existed excuse is restricted to a narrow range. In short, the international harmonisation of changed circumstances has not yet taken place and the debate around this theme continues, maybe even longer because of a series of rules in the Seoul Central District Court in relation to Knock-in Knock-out (KIKO) currency option contracts litigation cases.[115]

In the field of Over-The-Counter ('OTC') derivatives, Knock in, Knock out Currency option ('KIKO') contract is a kind of zero-cost option launched by the Bank of Korea for the purpose of reducing expenditures when Korea companies buy options to hedge foreign exchange risk. It is the most popular foreign exchange contract.

In 2008, the international financial crisis triggered sharp fluctuations in market factors such as exchange rates, interest rates and oil prices. The KRW depreciation involved this global downturn caused some Korean companies taking part in KIKO contracts suffered significant economic losses. Very significant economic losses forced Korean

[115]Lou Jianbo and Liu Yan, 'The impact of the doctrine of changed circumstances – from Korean court ruling on some KIKO cases' (1999) 5 Law and Business Studies 19 [楼建波,刘燕,情势变更原则对金融衍生品交易法律基础的冲击–以韩国法院对KIKO合约纠纷案 的裁决为例,《法商研究》1999年第5期。].

companies to go to the court to file legislation to terminate KIKO contracts.[116]

A few of these cases were upheld by Seoul Central District Court on the basis of changed circumstances, which caused uproar in the international financial derivatives trading market. The authority of the global trade association for OTC derivatives – International Swaps and Derivatives Association ('ISDA') – expressly announced their concerns on their official website over these awards: 'The court has set dangerous precedents disrupting the fundamental right to enforceability of contracts in the country', 'The Seoul Central District Court rulings could severely inhibit derivatives activity in Korea and in turn risk upsetting financial stability if these decisions are upheld and banks made wary of entering into financial contracts'. Keith Noyes, ISDA Regional Director, Asia Pacific even stated further that 'ISDA sees the Court's decisions as a possible result of a fundamental misconception that banks generate profits that are commensurate with the losses of their counterparties.'[117]

Korea is not the main shore of OTC derivatives, nor are the parties of the aforesaid KIKO cases internationally well-known, even the awards themselves are only the interim ruling of the district court in Soul, Korea. The reason why ISDA took such a serious attitude is that these decisions shake the basis of KIKO, even of financial derivatives.

In the article *The Existence of Futures Markets, Noisy Rational Expectations and Informational Externalities*[118], Sanford J Grossman stated that 'The Keynes-Hicks theory of commodity futures markets is that they provide a mechanism by which risk averse speculators insure other risk averse traders who hold (positive or negative) stocks of a commodity subject to price fluctuation'. That is, essentially, price fluctuation is the ground on which the commodity futures market exists. The instability of economics is the direct reason for the origin of financial derivatives, of which external and unpredictable conditions are the content.[119]

---

[116] Ibid.

[117] `http://www.isda.org/press/press040109.html`, accessed on 15th August 2012.

[118] SJ Grossman, 'The existence of Futures markets, Noisy Rational Expectations and Informational Externalities' [1977] 44(3) Rev Econ Stud 431.

[119] Simply summarized by the author according toLou Jianbo and Liu Yan, 'The impact of the doctrine of changed circumstances – from Korean court ruling on some KIKO cases' (1999) 5 Law and Business Studies 19, 24 [楼建波,刘燕,情势变

Accordingly, the foundation of the reasonability of the existence of derivatives is removed by applying the change of circumstance in case of change in price, vice-versa.

Is it possible to eliminate financial derivatives in China? The answer is negative. Indeed, on the contrary, financial derivatives are well emphasised and dramatically developed in China. The China Securities Commission (CSRC: `www.scrc.gov.cn`), the China Bank Regulatory Commission (CBRC: `www.cbrc.gov.cn`) and the People's Bank of China (PBC: `www.pbc.gov.cn`) are involved in derivatives regulation. In February 2004, the CBRC issued new rules concerning derivatives which abolished many of the restrictions that had previously been in place concerning the trading of derivatives.[120] Furthermore, in 2009, the Supreme People's Court through the foregoing guidance pointed out that when judges try cases related to contracts involving commodities whose prices have long been volatile, such as oil, coke non-ferrous metals and investment-oriented financial products like stocks and futures, the courts should discreetly apply the doctrine of changed circumstances.

Taking this fact into consideration it can be seen that the existence of financial derivatives is determined by the development of the economy and so it is inevitable in China.

As to the sanctity of contract, then, it is clear that China should not give it up because without doubt, it would directly expose China to dampening international investor confidence in derivatives and in turn increase risk, thereby ruining both the contract system and derivatives.

Therefore, there should be consistency between the sanctity of contract and derivatives from this perspective. The optimum way to cope with the conflicts between changed circumstances and financial derivatives is to exclude change in price from the principle of changed circumstances. This mechanism reflects the modern trend towards giving the court some power to moderate the rigours of freedom (changed circumstances) and sanctity of contract.

Compared to the aforementioned countries, one may ask: is it necessary to completely 'exclude' it? Can we keep it and modify the contract only in the case of extreme circumstances as in German or US law?

It is not a yes-no question in China for certain unavoidable problems.

更原则对金融衍生品交易法律基础的冲击–以韩国法院对KIKO合约纠纷案 的裁决为例,《法商研究》1999年第5期。].

[120] JC Hull, *Fundamentals of Futures and Options Markets Seventh Edition* (Pearson Press 2011).

Firstly, change in price, like inflation and currency fluctuation, is a kind of normal commercial risk now. Comparatively, under the self-sufficient dominant era, economics was restricted. Even during some particular periods, for example between the establishment of the PRC and the enforcement of the open policy in China, the economy still did not fully run along free-market economy principles. Market price always seems to be at the same level. Commercial is a term that is unknown to most people, not to mention commercial risk.

However, over the last three decades, great changes have happened. China has reverted to the international society, carrying out international trade, influencing and being influenced in many fields, particularly the economic field. Moreover, globalisation has further strengthened the uniform understanding of a large number of market principles and rules. Additionally, the baptism of the global financial crisis in 1997 stimulated people, especially business people's awareness of the truth that prices are always changing and they have to face up to this fact. In particular, the aforementioned guidance of the Supreme People's Court stated that commercial risks are the inherent risks associated with commercial activities, such as the relationship between supply and demand changes and price changes which are not yet extreme, whilst the change of circumstances is unforeseen and the non-market-system inherent risks.[121] That's why the new industries including forwards, futures, swaps enjoy such a rapid development. Based on the business person's common awareness of altering price, it is reasonable to say that change in price is a normal commercial risk rather than something that meets the requirement of changed circumstances.

Secondly, this objective is related to a modern conception of contract law in general and the role of judge therein.[122]

From the analysis in (A),(B),(C) and(D) it is possible to conclude something. Both the English law and the Germany laws take a strict view over the price change. However, the former only recognises disappearance of the contract rather than empowering the courts to revise the contract, which does not interfere with the freedom of the contract. While German law empowers the courts to terminate or revise the contract in case of severe changes in prices in order to achieve final

[121] Guidance of the Supreme People's Court of the PRC.

[122] H Rösler, 'Hardship in German Codified Private Law – In Comparative Perspective to English, French and International Contract Law' [2007] 15(4) ERPL 483, 509.

justice, which is similarly indicated by US law. Despite thses differences among these legal systems, one common thing they have is the judgment of 'degree' of fundamental change 'rely heavily on judicial interpretation'.[123]

Nonetheless, China is one of the codified countries, in which the sole criterion for judges to examine cases and make conclusion are the codified laws, rules and regulations or other legally enacted documents. Judges have no rights to create a new rule when judging a particular case. Provided that legislature determines to incorporate price changes which would be intervened by the courts by the means of applying changed circumstances, it can only be done by means of stating a clear starting line via the legislature. That is, the relevant legislative body should state a clear and uniform line for applying change of circumstances. For example, if the legislative body considers '5 times' is a reasonable marker, it should clearly state 'it is right to adapt the principle of changed circumstances when the prices are 5 times or even more now than the disputing contract was concluded. Otherwise the contractual relationship should continue.'

Nevertheless, at present, Chinese law lacks such uniform line dividing normal and extreme price change and no detailed clarification pressed in the form of laws, or rules and regulations but a notice provided on 7th July 2009, two months after the Contract Law Interpretation (II) came into force. The Supreme People's Court issued this notice giving guidance on the trial of a number of issues concerning civil and commercial contract disputes in the current global-crisis-situation (guidance),[124] which emphasised that the principle of changed circumstances should be carefully applied. In addition, it emphasised that the courts should follow the principle of focusing on the protection of the observant party. It may be helpful, but it is obvious that this single guidance is not enough to guide such a subtle and significant area.

In addition, from these previously analysed cases it is clear that every case has its own unique background and all of them are determined on a 'case-by-case' basis.[125] It is not possible or reasonable to

---

[123] Ibid., 507.

[124] Guidance of the Supreme People's Court of the PRC, `http://www.court.gov.cn/qwfb/sfwj/yj/201002/t20100224_1931.htm`, accessed 10th July 2012.

[125] Cf H Veytia, 'The Requirement of Justice and Equity in Contracts' [1995] 69 Tul L Rev 1191, in which a currency devaluation of more than 50% is considered as a fundamental manner of change; Cf SW Hubbard, 'Relief from Burdensome Long-term Contracts: Commercial Impracticability, Frustration of Purpose, Mutual

determine an exact number or draw a uniform line. Consequently, the intention of including price change into the doctrine of *rebus sic stantibus* is meaningless.

Thirdly, giving such a high degree of discretion to the judiciary to modify the contracts may create the very defects that they seek to cure, vagueness and insecurity in contractual relationship. 'The contract is the law of the parties'.[126] When a contract imposes successive payments on a debtor for a certain duration, it is because the creditor had wanted to guarantee the payments against all later eventualities and particularly against the variation of prices.[127] The sanctity of a contract is manifested in a party's absolute liability for obligations assumed thereunder. One should bear the risk if one wants to gain benefit. Furthermore, because of the uncertainty of the futures, to some extent the purpose of a contract is to clarify the expectations of the present and future of the contractual relationship because 'a contract is not merely a momentary picture of reality as it existed at the point of formation because it also initiates and covers events that develop in the future'.[128] Admittedly, 'the court will not improve the contract which the parties have made for themselves, however desirable the improvement might be'.[129] The revision of contracts by a judge runs contrary to the respect accorded a contractual commitment and the economic utility of the contract.

Mistake of Fact, and Equitable Adjustment' [1982] 47 Mo L Rev 79, 91: Hubbard indicated that 'While no exact standard exists, relief has been denied when a 100% cost increase was involved.'

[126] Article 1134 Napoleonic Code.

[127] H Veytia, 'The Requirement of Justice and Equity in Contracts' [1995] 69 Tul L Rev 1191, 1200.

[128] Ibid.

[129] Trollope & Colls Ltd v North West Metropolitan Regional Hospital Board [1973] 1 WLR 601 at 609 by Pearson LJ.

F. Conclusion

In the introduction, the question was asked whether the change in price should be excluded from the reasons which call for the application of change of circumstances in China.

The principle of *pacta sunt servanda* is undoubtedly the essential foundation of the market system. Contracts become binding by the mere consent of the parties, except for those contracts that must have a form established by law. From the time a contract becomes binding, the promisors are strictly liable for breach of their contractual duties[130] in accordance with the traditional contract doctrine, that is, the contracting parties are obligated not only to perform that which has been expressly agreed to, but also are liable for the consequences that, by the nature of the contract, conform with the principle of good faith, custom and usage or the law.[131]

Both in continental Europe and in common law countries in the 20th century, change of conditions have been reintroduced in order to safeguard justice and equity. In some cases the disadvantaged parties are discharged from continuing the performance without the consequence of bearing damages on the basis of the theory of changed circumstances. Furthermore, in certain countries and cases it is also not impossible to obtain a court-imposed price adjustment so as to ensure the extra costs imposed by the unforeseen change in price are born equitably by the parties, thereby re-establishing the balance within the contract.

The relation between change in price and change of conditions, however, is still a subtle sphere not only in most individual countries, but also to the international organisations, not mention the price adjust-

[130] Cf Restatement (Second) of Contracts, Chapter 11, Introductory Note, 1981.

[131] H Veytia, 'The Requirement of Justice and Equity in Contracts' [1995] 69 Tul L Rev 1191, 1199.

ment system. It cannot be denied that though contractual obligations are considered no longer absolute and the dicta of *rebus sic stantibus* obviously developed after the disappearance of almost one hundred years. Due to the severe influence caused by World Wars on commercial contracts, the course of the development of this doctrine is very tortuous.[132] In addition1, even these countries adopted this principle always 'for many reasons, historically have limited the availability of this doctrine to very narrow circumstances'. In relation to change in price, the application of the doctrine of changed circumstances is 'hardly never'[133] or 'the courts [...] almost without exception have refused to grant any relief when the promisor's sole complaint has been increased cost of performance'[134] in Germany or 'increased cost, alone cannot constitute commercial impracticability'[135] in the USA.

To follow the international trend of accepting changed circumstance is beneficial for China in order to fully understand the uniform rules and take advantage of more opportunities. It is true that the modification way represents the most flexible and extensive model.[136] But one of the motivating factors which ordinarily induces the promise to enter into a fixed price contract is to lock in his own cost of performance; thus, to discharge the promisor due to change in price or its increased cost of performance would frustrate the primary purpose of the promise in making the contract in the first place.[137] Consequently, part of the English way is intrinsically preferable to China: adhering to the contract rather than taking a broad interpretation of frustration which would contradict the parties' shared expectations. It is good to maintain the stability of business relationship in a developing background.

---

[132]Some countries, eg France, never accepted the theory of changed circumstances in civil law.

[133]H Rösler, 'Changed and unforeseen circumstances in German and international contract law', [2008] 5 SLR 47.

[134]SW Hubbard, 'Relief from Burdensome Long-term Contracts: Commercial Impracticability, Frustration of Purpose, Mutual Mistake of Fact, and Equitable Adjustment' [1982] 47 Mo L Rev 79-80. Hubbard also indicates at page 91 that 'While no exact standard exists, relief has been denied when a 100% cost increase was involved. A 1000% cost increase, however, has been held sufficient to support a finding of impracticability.'

[135]S 2-615 UCC, Official Comment 4.

[136]H Rösler, 'Hardship in German Codified Private Law – In Comparative Perspective to English, French and International Contract Law' [2007] 15(4) ERPL 483, 507.

[137]TR Hurst, 'Inflation, Deflation and Long Term Contractual Relationships Under UCC Section 2-615' [1990] 95 Com LJ 290, 296.

Whereas a broad interpretation of changed circumstances, change in price like the abovementioned case, would make the businessmen rely heavily on arbitrarily making use of this theory and improperly escaping from their obligations that they should perform or have promised even without careful thought whenever to perform is more difficult than one could foresee at the moment of the conclusion of the contract, which will undoubtedly 'defeat their apparent objectives'.[138]

On the other hand, we have to take into account the fact that relevant fields around change in price and change of circumstance still need much more improvement. For example, we have no Law Reform (Frustrated Contracts) Act 1943 in English law or bank system related to price evaluation mechanism in German law. It is thus no wise to focus on expanding the availability of this doctrine, regardless of the defects of the present law system and importance of maintaining the sanctity of contract in the long run. To introduce the issue of change in price into a contract would be to undermine or destroy the certainty of the contract and the parties' expectations of certainty of performance and cause new instability into economic life, which runs contrary to the original purpose of achieving justice by means of incorporating change in price into changed circumstances.

To sum up, hence, the optimum solution from both the economic and legal point of views is to exclude change in price from changed circumstances in China.

[138]ME Dickste, 'Revitalizing the international law governing concession agreement' [1988] 6 INT'L TAX & BUS L 54.

G. Reference List

I. Cases

Aluminium Company of America v Essex Group Inc [1980] 499 F Supp 53 (WD Pa)

Arcos v Ronaasen [1933] AC 470

British Movietonews v London and District Cinemas [1952] AC 166

Cook v Deltona Corp [1985] 753 F 2d 1552 (11th Cir)

City of Vernon v City of Los Angeles [1955] 45 Cal 2d 710, 290 P 2d 841

Davis Contractors Ltd v Fareham UDC [1956] AC 696

Dillon v United States [1957] 156 F Supp 719 (Ct Cl)

Eleventh Circuit in Cook v Deltona Corp [1985] 753 F 2d 1552 (11th Cir)

Gore District Council v Power Co Limited [1996] 1 NZLR 58

Hyde v The Dean of Windsor [1597] Cro Eliz 552, 78 Eng Rep 798

Iowa Elec Light & Power Co [1978] 467 F Supp 129

Krell v Henry [1903] 2 KB 740

Liamco v Libya, 12th April 1977, Yearbook Commercial Arbitration (1981)

Mineral Park Land v Howard [1916] 172 Cal 289, 156 P 458

Multiservice Bookbinding Ltd v Marden [1979] Ch 84

National Carriers Ltd v Panalpina Northern Ltd [1981] AC 675

Philips Hong Kong Ltd v Attorney General of Hong Kong (1993) 61 BLR 41

RGZ 103, 328

Staffordshire Area Health Authority v South Staffordshire Water Works Co [1978] All ER 769

Taylor v Caldwell [1863] 122 ER 309

Trollope & Colls Ltd v North West Metropolitan Regional Hospital Board [1973] 1 WLR 601

Wates Ltd v Greater London Council (1983) 25 BLR 1 (CA)

Westminster v Clarke [1536] Dyer 276, pl 186, 73, Eng Rep 59, 63

Williams v Floyd [1863] W Jones 179, 82 Eng Rep 309

Wuhan Gas Company (WGC) v Chongqing Testing Instrument Factory (CTIF) [1992]

II. Legislation

Contract Law of the People's Republic of China

German Civil Code [*Bürgerliches Gesetzbuch, BGB*]

ISDA, http://www.isda.org/press/press040109.html

Law Reform (Frustrated Contracts) Act 1943,
http://www.legislation.gov.uk/ukpga/Geo6/6-7/40

Napoleonic Code [*Code Napoléon*]

Restatement (Second) of Contracts,
http://www.lexisnexis.com/lawschool/study/outlines/html/contracts/index.asp

Uniform Commercial Code (UCC)

The Supreme People's Court's Interpretation of Certain Issues Concerning the Application of the Contract Law,
http://www.court.gov.cn/qwfb/sfjs/201002/t20100210_1051.htm

The Supreme People's Court, 'Minutes on 1993 National Symposium on Trials of Economic Cases', May 6, 1993 Fa Fa (1993) No. 81

UNIDROIT Principles

III. Secondary Sources

Burrows A, *Understanding the law of Obligations: 'Dividing the Law of Obligations'* (Hart Publishing 1998)

Beale H, Fauvarque-cosson B, Rutgers J, Tallon D and Vogenauer S, *Cases, Materials and Text on Contract Law* (2nd edn, Hart Publishing 2010)

Beale H and Lando O, *Principles of European Contract Law, Parts I and II* (Kluwer Law International Press 2000)

Cheng S, 'Change of Circumstances and Chinese Contract Law system – From the point of the application of Article 26 of Contract Law Interpretation II of the PRC' [2012] 6 Journal of Law Application [程顺增,论情势变更制度与我国合同法体系之契合–以最高法院《关于适用〈中华人民共和国合同法〉若干问题的解释（二）》第26条的适用为视角,法律适用,2012年第6期]

Coote B, *Contract as Assumption* (Hart Publishing 2010)

Dawson JP, 'Judicial Revision of Frustrated Contracts' [1983] 63 BUL Rev 1039

Dickste ME, 'Revitalizing the international law governing concession agreement' [1988] 6 INT'L TAX & BUS L 54

Farnsworth A, *Contracts* (Little, Brown 1982)

Gallo P, 'Changed Conditions and Problems of Price Adjustment. An Historical and Comparative analysis' [1998] 6 ERPL 285

Garner BS, *Black's Law Dictionary* (5th edn, West Pub Co 1979)

Gordley J and von Mehren AT, *An introduction to the Comparative Study of Private Law: Readings, Cases, Materials* (Cambridge University Press 2006)

Gregory P and Stuart R, *Comparing Economic Systems in the Twenty-First Century* (7th edn, South-Western College Pub 2003)

Grossman S, 'The existence of Futures markets, Noisy Rational Expectations and Informational Externalities' [1977] 44(3) Rev Econ Stud 431

Hawkland WD, 'The Energy Crisis and Section 2-615 of the Uniform Commercial Code' [1974] 79 Com LJ 75

Hay P, 'Frustration and its Solution in German Law' [1961] 10(4) Am J Comp Law 345

Hogg M, *Promises and Contract law: comparative perspectives* (Cambridge University Press 2011)

Hubbard SW, 'Relief from Burdensome Long-term Contracts: Commercial Impracticability, Frustration of Purpose, Mutual Mistake of Fact, and Equitable Adjustment' [1982] 47 Mo L Rev 79

Hull JC, *Fundamentals of Futures and Options Markets Seventh Edition* (Pearson Press 2011)

Hurst TR, 'Inflation, Deflation and Long Term Contractual Relationships Under UCC Section 2-615' [1990] 95 Com LJ 290

Kong X, *Comments and Theoretical Study on Difficult Cases of the Contract Law* (Revised edn, People's Court Press 2000)

Leclercq H, 'Force Majeure in Chinese Commercial law' [1989] 7 J Energy & Nat Resources L 238

Li G, 'Shen Jiaben Nianpuchangbian' (Taibei, Chengwen Press 1992) [李贵连,《沈家本年谱长编》,(台北, 成文出版社,1992)]

Lou J and Liu Y, 'The impact of the doctrine of changed circumstances – from Korean court ruling on some KIKO cases' (1999) 5 Law and Business Studies 19

[楼建波,刘燕,情势变更原则对金融衍生品交易法律基础的冲击–以韩国法院对KIKO合约纠纷案 的裁决为例,《法商研究》1999年第5期。]

Maskow D, 'Hardship and Force Majeure' [1992] 40 Am J Comp L 657

McKendrick E, *Chitty on contracts – General principles* (Sweet & Maxwell 2004)

Peel E and Treitel GH, *The Law of Contract* (12th edn, Sweet & Maxwell 2007)

Ringwood A, 'Terminating a Contract' [1996] NZLJ 204

Rösler H, 'Hardship in German Codified Private Law – In Comparative Perspective to English, French and International Contract Law' [2007] 15(4) ERPL 483

Idem., 'Changed and unforeseen circumstances in German and international contract law', [2008] 5 SLR 47

Schmitt MA and Wollschlager BA, 'Commercial Impracticability: Making the Impracticable Practicable' (1976) 81 Com LJ 9

Shi S, *The Law of Obligation* (China University of Political Science and Law Press January 2000)

[史尚宽,《债法总论》,中国政法大学,2000年1月]

Sun L, *Selection of Legislative Materials of the Contract Law of the People's Republic of China* (Law Press 1999)

Stevenson Conrad L, 'Bernina Distributors, Inc. v Bernina Sewing Machine Co.: New Grounds for Commercial Impracticability Based on Currency Exchange Rates under Uniform Commercial Code Section 2-615' [1983] NCJ Int'l L & Com Reg 117

Treitel GH, *Frustration and Force Majeure* (2nd edn, Sweet & Maxwell 2004)

Veytia H, 'The Requirement of Justice and Equity in Contracts' [1995] 69 Tul L Rev 1191

Walter P, 'Commercial Impracticability in Contracts' [1987] 61(2) St John's L Review 225

Zhang T, 'On the Limit to the Principle of Changes in Situation' [1996] 5 Hebei Law

[张坦,论对情势变更原则的限制,河北法学,1996年第5期]

FSC
www.fsc.org
MIX
Papier aus verantwortungsvollen Quellen
Paper from responsible sources
FSC® C105338